# EXTINCT AMPHIBIANS

## and those in danger of extinction

## Philip Steele

**Franklin Watts**

London  New York  Sydney  Toronto

© 1991 Zoe Books Limited

Devised and produced by
Zoe Books Limited
15 Worthy Lane
Winchester
Hampshire SO23 7AB
England

First published in 1991
in Great Britain by
Franklin Watts Ltd
96 Leonard Street
London EC2A 4RH

First published in Australia by
Franklin Watts Australia
14 Mars Road
Lane Cove
New South Wales 2066

ISBN 0 7496 0591 X

A CIP catalogue record for this book is
available from the British Library.

Printed in the United Kingdom

Consultant: Professor Richard T. J. Moody,
BSc, Dip Ed, PhD, FGS
Design: Julian Holland Publishing Ltd
Picture researcher: Jennifer Johnson
Illustrator: Robert Morton

**Photograph acknowledgements**

p12 Jane Burton/Bruce Coleman Ltd,
p13 Jack Dermid/Bruce Coleman Ltd,
p18 G I Bernard/Oxford Scientific Films,
p19 David Woodfall/NHPA, p20 Atsushi
Sakurai/Orion Press/Bruce Coleman Ltd,
p24 Jane Burton/Bruce Coleman Ltd,
p26 Mark N Boulton/Bruce Coleman Ltd,
p27 Michael Freeman/Bruce Coleman Ltd.

# Contents

# Extinct frogs

Las Vegas is a city in the middle of a desert in North America, where there is a rainfall of only 112 mm (4.5 in) a year. People need water, and the city planners had to make use of every water source available to them. Springs were tapped and the water piped to the city. To the west, the Colorado River was dammed to form large reservoirs which also supply the city.

**The Vegas Valley Leopard Frog**
The damper parts of the Vegas Valley had been home to a rare kind of leopard frog. The re-routing of the waterways destroyed the places where it lived, or its habitat. Fish were also introduced into ponds and springs, where they preyed on the leopard frog's spawn and tadpoles. During the 1930s, sightings of the Vegas Valley Leopard Frog became fewer and fewer and by 1966 scientists think it had probably become extinct, and would be seen no more.

1940  Palestinian Painted Frog discovered.
1942  Vegas Valley Leopard Frog probably disappearing.
1956  Palestinian Painted Frog probably extinct.
1966  Vegas Valley Frog probably extinct.

▼ A Vegas Valley Leopard Frog. Although leopard frogs get their name because of their spotted skins, Vegas Valley Leopard Frogs had only pale spots and some had no spots at all. They also lacked the white stripe on their jaws that other leopard frogs have.

## The Palestinian Painted Frog

The Hula Valley is in the north-east of Israel, on the border with Syria. The Jordan River flows into the Hula Valley from the north and continues to the Sea of Galilee. The valley used to be a lake, but part of it has now been drained by the Israelis and turned into farmland. To prevent the spread of the disease malaria, they also drained the swamps where the malaria-carrying mosquitos lived, and introduced fish into the lake so that they would eat the mosquito eggs.

The changes to the environment helped the local people, but did great harm to the Palestinian Painted Frog. It needed the shallow swamps in order to survive.

▲ The Palestinian Painted Frog was about 8 cm (3 in) long. Its blotched back was ochre and rust-coloured, and its stomach was black. The front legs of the Palestinian Painted Frog were much longer than those of other painted frogs. The frog was known from very few specimens, and its extinction is now listed as "virtually certain" by the International Union for the Conservation of Nature and Natural Resources (IUCN).

DID YOU KNOW?
● When the Palestinian Painted Frog was discovered, two were captured and kept in captivity. One ate the other!

# From water to land

About 380 million years ago, the first amphibians began to appear on Earth. Their ancestors were bony fish whose fins had developed into limbs. The new creatures still needed water to breed.

Later, some amphibians developed further and evolved into reptiles that could live entirely on land. Other early amphibians developed into the amphibians we know today.

AMPHIBIANS
- Amphibians are animals whose lives are suited to two very different worlds – water and dry land.
- Some amphibians spend a part of their lives in lakes or rivers, breathing through gills, and the rest of their lives on land, breathing air into their lungs or absorbing it through their moist skin.
- Amphibians are cold-blooded creatures. This means that their body heat changes with the temperature of their surroundings.

▼ The first amphibian we know much about was called *Ichthyostega*. When *Ichthyostega* was alive, the landmass that today makes up Greenland lay near the Equator, where the weather was warm. *Ichthyostega* probably moved slowly on land, but travelled more easily in water where it hunted fish.

*Ichthyostega* was about 1 m (3 ft) long. Its legs were short and strong. Its fish-like origins can be seen in its tail fin and in the small remnant of what in fish is a bony gill cover. Its snout was rounded and less developed than in most amphibians.

▲ Although its long body and powerful tail make *Crassigyrinus* look like a fish, it did have weak limbs and was an early amphibian. *Crassigyrinus* was 2 m (6 ft) long from snout to tail and fed on other water creatures. Fossils of this amphibian were first found 60 years ago.

DID YOU KNOW?
- The Greek word *amphibios* means a "double life".
- Amphibians were the first land animals with backbones.
- The great age of amphibian evolution occurred between 350 and 285 million years ago. At that time, much of the Earth was covered in swamps and forests.
- There are about 2400 amphibian species surviving today. These include frogs and toads, newts and salamanders, and the worm-like apodans.

360 million years ago: *Ichthyostega* evolves.
330 million years ago: *Crassigyrinus* alive.

# Fossils

We know about amphibians that lived hundreds of millions of years ago because many remains have been found. These traces of prehistoric animals have survived because when a creature died, its body sank quickly into soft mud or sediment. The soft part of the body rotted away, leaving behind the hard parts or skeleton.

The skeletons of amphibians were often pressed into the mud of swamps and ponds and preserved. The bones, and sometimes even tadpoles, eggs, muscles, skin or footprints, were buried by more mud and rock. They were pressed and hardened until they became fossils.

Later, movements of the Earth's crust exposed the rocks and fossils they contained. People sometimes find fossils when the ground is being dug before a road is built.

▼ During the twentieth century, fossils of *Seymouria* have been discovered in the south western American states of Oklahoma, Texas, Utah and New Mexico. The fossils show that *Seymouria's* skull and teeth are typically amphibian, but its spine and limbs are very like those of the reptiles. *Seymouria* measured 70 cm (2 ft) from nose to tail.

## Diplocaulus

The strangest-looking amphibian ever known was called *Diplocaulus.* Many remains, including those of its young, have been found in Texas, in the USA. Its body was like a salamander's, and because of the shape of its legs and head scientists think that it lived on the bottom of lakes where it hunted fish.

▲ *Diplocaulus* was about 80 cm (2.5 ft) long with a flattened skull that was 20 cm (8 in) wide.

DID YOU KNOW?
- The largest amphibian ever known was probably *Prionosuchus plummeri* which measured 9 m (30 ft) in length. Fossil remains were found in Brazil in 1972.
- In 1726 a fossil discovered in Germany was declared to be the skeleton of a child who had died in the great flood described in the Bible. In 1811 the "child skeleton" was recognized as a fossil of an extinct giant salamander. It was named *Andrias scheuchzeri.*

270 million years ago: *Diplocaulus* alive.
260 million years ago: *Seymouria* alive.
230 million years ago: *Prionosuchus plummeri* alive.
10 million years ago: *Andrias scheuchzeri* alive.

# Times of change

Over millions of years, the living conditions on Earth altered. The climate changed from one period to another, and with it the vegetation. Animals that did not manage to adapt to these changes became extinct. Many creatures had to evolve in order to survive.

220 million years ago: *Triadobatrachus* alive. 200 million years ago: *Mastodonsaurus* alive.

## Mastodonsaurus

This giant amphibian of the prehistoric world lived in pools and swamps. It fed on fish which it seized with the pointed teeth in its long jaw. Despite its large size, *Mastodonsaurus* had small, weak legs and was poorly suited to a life on land. Most of its time was spent in the water, and it was unable to survive periods of drought.

◀ Remains of *Triadobatrachus* were found in Madagascar in 1936. They showed that the amphibian was only 12 cm (5 in) long. *Triadobatrachus* had a head like a frog's head of today, but its legs and body were less frog-like. By comparing the skeletons of extinct amphibians, scientists can work out how they evolved. For example, it would seem from *Triadobatrachus* that amphibians' skulls became frog-like before the rest of their bodies.

▲ *Mastodonsaurus* was
about 4 m (13 ft) long,
with a frog-like body and
a long flattened head.

# Under threat

Over many millions of years, all kinds of amphibians have evolved and become extinct. The natural world always had enough food and water to sustain new species. However, the development of human beings on Earth has changed the pace of evolution.

The main threat to amphibians comes from the damage that humans do to the environment. Wetlands have been drained, streams polluted and tropical forests cut down. All these places are home to amphibian species, which need moist habitats in order to survive.

Amphibians are also threatened by hunting. They are eaten by birds, reptiles and fish, but they are also hunted by humans. In some parts of the world, salamanders are eaten for food. Elsewhere frogs are eaten, but usually only the back legs which are often served cooked in garlic.

◀ A male Great Crested Newt. The Great Crested Newt is now a protected species in the British Isles. The draining of land for farming and building has destroyed its habitat.

Newts breed in April and lay their eggs in May. The tadpoles, or efts, grow into adults and leave the water in July. They spend the autumn on land and then hibernate for the winter.

◀ A large adult Spotted Salamander. The numbers of Fire or Spotted Salamanders are declining because of the effect of humans on their habitats. Chemicals from factory chimneys, and exhaust fumes from cars rise into the air and later fall as acid rain. This has poisoned the lakes of western Europe where young salamanders have been killed as they develop.

Humans use frogs in other ways too. Some frogs are poisonous, and in South America they are hunted so that the poison can be smeared on arrow-tips. Large numbers of frogs are also used for dissection and laboratory experiments.

DID YOU KNOW?
- The scientific name for frogs and toads is Anura, which means "without a tail".
- Anura are animals which mostly move by leaping or hopping. Some spend most of their lives in water, while others have adapted to a land-based life.
- The scientific name for long-bodied amphibians, such as newts and salamanders, is Caudata. This means "having a tail".

THE FIRE WALKER
- People used to think that salamanders were able to walk through fire without being damaged. Salamanders were even thrown into fires as people thought that they would put out the flames. Unfortunately, the salamanders died in vain, as the belief was untrue.

# Frogs and toads

About 30 species of frogs and toads are at risk around the world. The threat to these creatures has come mainly from loss of habitat. Forests have been cut down for timber, and this is a major threat because over three-quarters of all frog species live in the tropical rain forests. Rivers and streams have been piped and channelled, or dammed, in order to carry water to crops or to supply houses. The banks of ponds have been cut back and cleared of vegetation to allow people to fish more easily.

Acid rain poisons ponds and streams, making it impossible for frogs and toads to breed in them. Another threat is the chemicals used by farmers to kill insect pests. The frogs are killed when they eat the poisoned insects or when the pesticides seep directly into the water where they live.

▼ The largest frog in the world is the Goliath, which lives in deep river pools in the West African states of Cameroon and Equatorial Guinea. It has been known to have a body length of 35 cm (14 in), not including the limbs which are the same length again. It can weigh over 3 kg (6.5 lb). The Goliath is on the IUCN list of the world's most vulnerable species.

◄ The Italian Agile Frog is another species that is under serious threat of becoming endangered. It lives in damp woodland in southern Switzerland, northern Italy and Yugoslavia. It is very like the more common Agile Frog, but its belly is pinkish rather than yellow and its ear-drum is smaller. The Italian Agile Frog is about 7 cm (3 in) in length.

AMPHIBIAN DEFENCES
- The traditional enemies of amphibians are reptiles, birds and fish. Frogs and toads have developed many weapons to protect themselves. They are often camouflaged so that they cannot be seen. Some puff up their bodies to confuse an enemy, and others roll over and pretend to be dead. Many have poisonous skins which protect them from predators. Some frogs have brightly coloured skins which warn off other creatures.
- Frogspawn and tadpoles are easily eaten by fish, and so many frog and toad species carry their eggs or their young with them, glued to their legs or hidden in folds in the skin.

DID YOU KNOW?
- The eye of the Goliath Frog is as big as a human's.
- An Agile Frog can leap over a distance of 2 m (6 ft) and can clear a height of 0.75 m (2.5 ft).

# Island species

Remote islands are often home to unique species. They have adapted to a very specialized habitat and can thrive in no other place. For this reason their numbers remain very low. When people have settled on the islands, they have cut down trees and built houses. This has reduced the number of places where the island animals can live. People also often brought dogs, cats and rats with them which hunted the island species.

The Seychelles is a group of islands in the Indian Ocean. They provided an ideal place for animal species to live until the islands became populated. Tourism and farming opened up the countryside and as a result some bird and reptile species became extinct. Today four species of amphibian unique to the Seychelles are listed as threatened. They include the Seychelles Tree Frog, and three other related species: Thomasset's Seychelles Frog, Gardiner's Seychelles Frog and the Seychelles Frog.

## The Seychelles Frog

This rare amphibian hunts for insects and other small creatures amongst the fallen leaves on the forest floor. It lays its spawn on damp soil. When the tadpoles hatch out, they are carried about on the moist skin of their mother's back. This ensures that the young do not dry out. The Seychelles Frog gradually evolved these characteristics in order to survive in a particular habitat. Recent changes to the environment have given the frog no time to adapt.

▶ The Seychelles are home to several long-legged, green or brown frogs which are found nowhere else. Thomasset's Seychelles Frog (top right), the Seychelles Frog (centre and bottom right), and Gardiner's Seychelles Frog (bottom left) all measure between 20 and 25mm (0.7 and 0.9 in) in length.

The Seychelles Tree Frog (top left) is also found on Madagascar and the African mainland. It has special suction pads on its toes which help it to cling to leaves. It measures between 20 and 80mm (0.7 and 3 in).

All these Seychelles frogs are under threat and further work needs to be done to find out how many survive.

---

DID YOU KNOW?
● Tadpoles of the Seychelles Frog have no gills. Instead they breathe through tiny holes in their skin.

# The Natterjack story

The Natterjack Toad is found in western, central and eastern Europe, and is common in France and Spain. In the British Isles, however, the Natterjack is disappearing fast.

The British Natterjacks will only live in warm sandy places, and like brackish ponds for breeding. This is unusual, because most amphibians do not like salty water.

Natterjacks are only found amongst coastal dunes and on heathland. During the twentieth century many dunes have been destroyed to make way for tourist sites, and the heathlands of southern England have been drained to build roads and housing estates. The Natterjack Toads have become rarer and rarer.

▼ The Natterjack Toad is normally about 8 cm (3 in) long, not including the limbs. It has a yellow stripe running down its back.

## Saving the Natterjack

When scientists realized that the survival of the Natterjack in Britain was under threat, they took action. Volunteers dug and improved breeding pools on nature reserves. Plans to build houses, drain land or plant forests were carefully checked. The fight for the survival of the Natterjack Toad will be a long one.

▲ During the breeding season, the male Natterjack calls to the female with a rattling croak. While it is calling the voice sac swells. The Natterjack has the loudest croak of all the European frogs.

DID YOU KNOW?
- Strict laws have been passed in Britain which make it illegal even to handle a Natterjack Toad without a special licence.
- During the twentieth century, 90 per cent of British sand dunes and heaths have disappeared.
- In Britain, 80 per cent of the Natterjack's breeding sites have been destroyed in the last 100 years.

# Giant salamanders

The largest amphibians surviving in the world today live in Asia. They are close relatives of the extinct salamander *Andrias scheuchzeri,* whose remains were discovered in Germany in the eighteenth century.

The Chinese Giant Salamander lives in the cold streams and marshes of China. The Japanese Giant Salamander also lives in cold streams, in the mountains of Japan. Fast-flowing water supplies them with plenty of oxygen. These two species of giant salamander are normally about 1 m (3 ft) long, and weigh about 12 kg (26 lb). However, both have been known to exceed 1.5 m (5 ft) and weigh more than 40 kg (88 lb).

The Chinese and Japanese Giant Salamanders are in danger of becoming extinct. The Chinese is listed as "threatened" and the Japanese is "very rare". Both are hunted for food and caught by fishermen.

◄ With its wrinkled body and flattened head, the Japanese Giant Salamander looks like a prehistoric monster. The folds on its body help it to absorb oxygen from the water. It stays submerged most of the time, surfacing only to breathe air into its lungs occasionally. Only the young have gills. The colour of its skin helps camouflage it amongst the boulders of mountain streams, where it snaps up prey such as snails and insects with a sideways motion.

DID YOU KNOW?
- The Japanese Giant Salamander is the world's longest-living amphibian. In captivity, it is known to have lived for over 51 years.
- The Chinese and Japanese Salamanders are related to the Hellbender, the largest North American Salamander.
- The Alpine Salamander takes four years to produce her young — longer than any other land creature. This black-skinned amphibian lives under boulders high in the Swiss Alps.

▲ The Chinese Giant Salamander looks very like the Japanese species. However its tail is shorter and its body is bulkier. Its head is huge and it has no eyelids.

# The Olm

In 1875 a salamander was discovered in a cave in what is now Yugoslavia. It had never been described in any scientific journal and was unknown in museums of natural history. It was called the Olm.

The Olm lives deep in limestone caves and in cool underground lakes and streams, where it feeds on small creatures such as water fleas. By the time the Olm is 18 months old, its dark skin has become pale and white in the darkness. Its eyes are blind and covered with skin.

The Olm is an unusual creature. A frog's tadpoles take oxygen directly from the water through gills, but develop lungs when they become adults. The Olm, however, never grows into a truly adult form. It lives in water and never comes on to dry land. It has long, feathery gills. The blood inside the gills gives them a reddish tinge. Nonetheless the Olm also has lungs and cannot survive without surfacing for air.

▶ The Olm has an eel-like body up to 30 cm (12 in) long. Its legs are small and weak, with three toes on the front feet and two on the rear.

DID YOU KNOW?
● The Mudpuppies of North America are also salamanders, and like the Olm they retain their dark red gills all their lives.

SURVIVAL AT RISK
The Olm lives in caves in the coastal region of Yugoslavia. It is also found at just one site in Italy. When a creature is as secretive as the Olm and lives underground, it is hard for scientists to find out details about its life. However, because the Olm has a very specialized lifestyle and can only be found in a few places, it has been placed on the list of threatened species prepared by the IUCN. The Olm is classed as "vulnerable". Water pollution or destruction of its habitat could prove to be a disaster to the whole species.

23

# Gills or lungs

As an amphibian grows up, its changes of form can be extreme. Just as tadpoles look very different in their larval form from the adult frogs or toads they will develop into, so do some species of salamander.

## The Axolotl

For many years scientists did not realize that the Axolotl was the same species as the Mexican Salamander, but at the larval stage of development. At this stage, the Axolotl has pink feathery gills and lives in lakes near Mexico City. However the Axolotl can lay eggs while in its larval form. If the lake dries up, the Axolotl turns into its adult form, breathing air. The Axolotl is now so rare that it is listed as a threatened species.

▼ The Axolotl is normally coloured brown with black spots, or black all over. Albino, or white, forms are fairly common also. Its body length is up to 18 cm (7 in), including a long, powerful tail. The Axolotl spends all its life in water and has feeble limbs.

## The Texas Blind Salamander

The Texas Blind Salamander was first discovered near San Marcos, in the American state of Texas. It lives underground in caves, wells and springs and is blind. It has no proper eyes. The head has a duck-like snout and leads to frond-like gills. This species of amphibian is unusual as it has no lungs in the adult stage.

▲ The Texas Blind Salamander looks like the European Olm, with a whitish skin and pink gills. Weak legs extend from a long, thin body.

The Texas Blind Salamander is listed as endangered on the IUCN's list of threatened species.

DID YOU KNOW?
- Fifteen species of salamander are at risk in the United States.
- Three salamander species are threatened in Mexico.

# Help the amphibians

Amphibians were an important group of animals in the prehistoric world. Today's amphibians are a small band of survivors. They deserve our special attention, because many of the places where they live are being destroyed.

Fortunately, people all over the world are trying to protect endangered animals. By studying rare amphibians to see how they live and breed, scientists can work out ways to protect them. Reserves are being established to protect the wetlands and heaths where amphibians live. Laws have been passed to prevent rare amphibians being traded or killed. It is also possible for you to take action in a simple but effective way. More and more people are building garden ponds to which newts and frogs can return each year to breed.

UNKNOWN SPECIES
● Three hundred years ago, 60 per cent of the world's surface was covered in forest. By the year 2000, only 25 per cent will be forested. It is possible that some species will become extinct before they have even been discovered.

◄ Warning: toads crossing! As toads return to their breeding pools, many are run over by cars. In some places, signs warn motorists of this seasonal hazard. In others, tunnels or pipes beneath the road help the toads make the journey unharmed.

▲ The Aransas National Wildlife Refuge lies amidst the lagoons, wetlands and oil wells of the Texas coast in the USA. It was founded in 1935, and is the perfect home for amphibians, including the Bullfrog, four species of leopard frog, six species of toad, and two species of salamander.

# Glossary

**acid rain** Rain mixed with poisonous chemicals given out by the smoke from factories and power stations.

**amphibian** An animal which has evolved so that part of its life is spent on the water, and part on the land.

**cold-blooded** Unable to control its own body temperature. Fish, reptiles and amphibians are cold-blooded. Birds and mammals are warm-blooded.

**dissection** Cutting apart for scientific examination.

**endangered** At risk of becoming extinct.

**environment** The world in which a plant or animal lives, including the soil, climate, vegetation and air.

**evolve** To develop or adapt over a long period. Creatures and plants evolve over millions of years as they adapt to changing living conditions.

**extinct** No longer living. Scientists now declare an animal to be officially extinct when it has not been seen in the wild for 50 years.

**fossil** The remains of an ancient animal or plant preserved in rock.

**gills** Organs which allow fish and amphibians to take in life-giving oxygen directly from the water.

**habitat** The place in which a particular plant or animal lives.

**herpetology** The scientific study of reptiles and amphibians.

**hibernation** The slowing down of the body or "sleep" during a period of cold weather.

**reptiles** Cold-blooded, egg-laying animals whose bodies are covered in plates or scales.

**spawn** The eggs of frogs or toads, often protected by a jellylike substance.

**species** A single group of identical animals or plants that can breed to produce like offspring.

**tadpole** The immature stage of a frog or toad; a swimming creature with gills.

**vulnerable** At risk of becoming an endangered species.

**wetlands** Regions of swamp, marsh, bog, ponds or pools.

# Find out more

- The study of amphibians and reptiles is called herpetology. Young herpetologists in the British Isles normally see only a few of these creatures. Warmer countries have a wider variety of amphibian life. The Common Frog is native to the British Isles and widespread. The Edible Frog, the large Marsh Frog and the tiny European Tree Frog have all been introduced, and are found only in very few places. The Common Toad is found in England and Scotland, and in parts of Wales and Ireland. The Natterjack Toad is becoming more rare. There are three British newts or salamanders: the widespread Smooth Newt, the Palmate Newt and the rare Great Crested or Warty Newt.

- Many zoos have collections of amphibians from other lands. Zoos are often the best places to see brilliantly coloured salamanders and exotic frogs. Find out if the zoo you visit is helping to breed any endangered species.

- Many museums have exhibits of fossils and reconstructions of prehistoric animals. Some of these will be amphibians, the ancestors of the dinosaurs. The Natural History section of the British Museum is in Cromwell Road, London SW7 5BD.

- Are you interested in helping to protect endangered amphibians around the world? The World Wide Fund for Nature has a junior membership. Contact Panda House, Weyside Park, Catteshall Lane, Godalming, Surrey GU7 1XR, for details of regional activities.

- Throughout England, Scotland, Wales and Ireland, there are local nature clubs and conservation trusts which organize activities and help protect nature reserves.

# Time chart

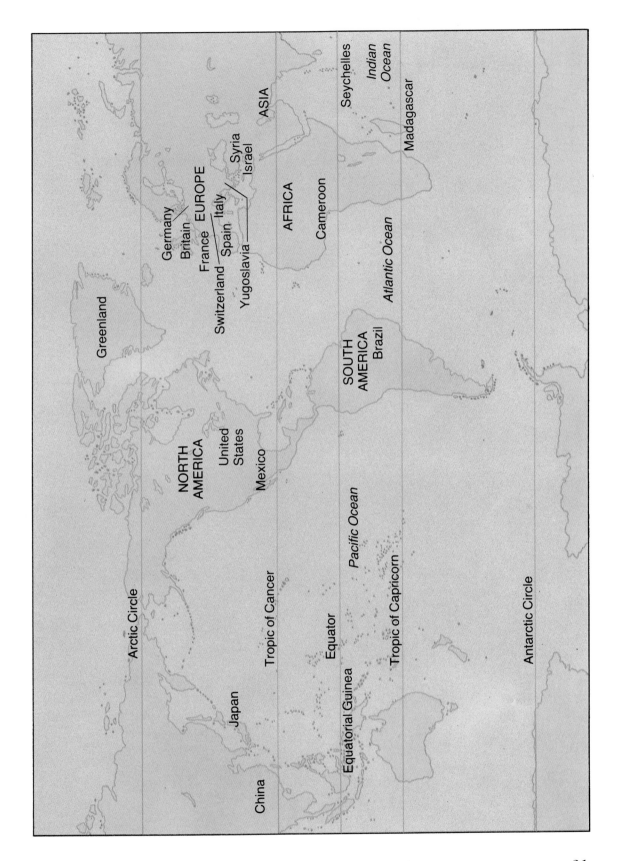

31

# Index